OTHER BOOKS BY MONIQUE R. RANSOM
A Father's Love
Who Is Thy Neighbor?

Unless otherwise indicated all Scripture quotations in this book are from the Authorized (The New King James) Version Copyright ©1994 by Thomas Nelson, Inc. Scriptures taken from the Holy Bible New International Version Copyright ©1993, 1978, and 1984 by International; Bible Society. Use by permission of Zondervan Publishing House. All rights reserved. Holy Bible, New Living Translation, Copyright © 1996. Used by permission of Tyndale House Publishers, Inc. Wheaton, Illinois 60189. All rights reserved, Definitions are quoted from Webster's new World Dictionary, Copy right ©1989, 1983, and 1979 by Simon and Schufter, Inc. Published by Western New World dictionary; A division of Simon and Schufter, Inc. 1 Gulf + Weston Plaza New York 10023. The Holman Bible Dictionary, Published by Broadman & Holman, 1991. All Rights Reserved. Used by permission of Broadman & Holman. Scripture quotations marked HCSB are taken from the Holman Christian Standard Bible®, Copyright © 1999, 2000, 2002, 2003, 2009 by Holman Bible Publishers. Used by permission. Holman Christian Standard Bible®, Holman CSB®, and HCSB® are federally registered trademarks of Holman Bible Publishers; Merriam-Webster's Collegiate Dictionary, Eleventh Edition copyright © 2008 by Merriam-Webster, Incorporated; Merriam-Webster Online Dictionary copyright © 2013 by Merriam-Webster, Incorporated.

Library of Congress-in-Publication Data:
Monique R. ransom
ISBN-13: 978-0615774428 (Custom)
ISBN-10: 0615774423

Copyright © 2013 Monique R. Ransom, a.k.a Monique Marshall, a.k.a Monique Marshall –Johnson. All Rights Reserved.
Edited By: Shawn Bramble
Published By Create Space Publishing

No parts of this book may be reproduced in whole or in part, or transmitted in any form without written permission from the author, except by a reviewer who may quote brief passages in a review; nor may any part of this book be reproduced, stored in a mechanical, photocopying, recording or other without written permission from the author or publication company. For information email Monique R. Marshall at shespeaks3@aol.com

A Twist of God's Word

CAN A CHRISTIAN BE POSSESSED BY AN EVIL SPIRIT?

Authored By

Monique R. Ransom

Prophetess

My People Suffer for Lack of Knowledge
Hosea 4:6

A Twist of God's Word

CAN A CHRISTIAN BE POSSESSED BY AN EVIL SPIRIT?

Authored By

Monique R. Ransom

Prophetess

Table of Content

Acknowledgement.. 10

Prelude... 13

Chapter 1- In the Beginning... 17

Chapter 2- Data Analysis..34

Chapter 3- A Ball of Confusion...................................37

Chapter 4- Data Analysis...61

Chapter 5- Tale of two Cities.....................................71

Chapter 6- Defining the Moments.............................76

Chapter 7- Possession vs. Oppression..................... 83

Chapter 8- Further Elaborations................................92

Chapter 9- The Meat and the Potatoes.................105

Chapter 10-The Finale...117

About The Author

Contact Information

Other Books by Author

Acknowledgements

I would like to thank all of you who made this book possible. It has been a long time coming but it is finally here.

I received so much encouragement and inspiration from my many people but especially my Best Friend, the David that was given to me by God, Sherian Keiko Anderson.

On every turn she has been there guiding and steering my path. I love her more than words can say. Since the time God stitched our hearts to one another it has been a journey. A journey, I could not have made without you. You are a gift to me and me to you that many have tried to destroy. No one can take your place ever because I have seen one of God's best.

To my children who have been in the trenches with me through great trials and tribulations, Still We Rise!

To my oldest, Renee, I want you to know that I admire you perseverance and your heart! You are an awesome you woman full of compassion and love.

You are a great mother to my grandchild Tyese and Aunt to Aaliyah. I know great things await you and I look forward to seeing these things come to pass in your life so I can laugh with you at the devil.

To my youngest Son Tyrone. You are such a joy to have around. Your calm demeanor and hopeful attitude has been an encouragement in my life. Great things and I mean great things are in your grasp. Just hold on and watch what God is going to do. You are wonderful, handsome and the best son anyone could wish for.

To my Baby Girl Sierra. No matter how you try to hide that hearts, it shows. I think that you are such a beautiful young woman inside and out. I still hold on to what God called said at birth, that you were born to worship Him. When you dance Heaven stand at attention and others see the anointing of God all over you. You are so gifted and talented beyond what you can imagine. Let God use you!

To my Dad, Bruce C. Ransom Jr. Ever since I told you that I was called by God, you stood by my side.

You encouraged me to write, speaker and saw the awesomeness that God had placed within me. You believe in the God in me and for that I could not Thank-you more.

To Mr. Shawn Bramble, Thank you for being my editor, my co-worker, and my friend who worked tirelessly in proofing this book for you. Heaven is your reward!

I don't know why God choose me but He did. I don't know why God loved me but He does. I don't know why God anointed me, but He has.

I am just glad God to serve Him. Lord I thank you most of all because without you this book and many other thing would not be. You saw the best in me when no one else did. You called me your friend and change my name to Lily!

I pray I live up to that name for your name sake.

PRELUDE

Now most of you viewing this book will wonder why I chose such a controversial topic. Well, it was not I, but Christ who inspired me to write about this issue which has become an overwhelming and alarming concern for today's church.

Why?

The title of this book is only one example of the gross injustice we have done with God's Word. One twist of God's Word can lead us to the misconceptions and the lack of understanding of who we serve, as well as how we should truly serve God.

God's Word in John 4:24 says that God is a Spirit and them that worship Him, MUST worship God in Spirit and truth. To Worship God in truth means to simply worship Him accord to His Word in the Bible. Truth that is corrupted and served with leaven, leavens the whole lump. That lump begins to affect our walk, our talk, and our overall perception of the One True Living God and His purpose for mankind on the earth.

Worship is more than the songs we sing at church, in our car, or in our home, it's a lifestyle of sacrifice! What is true worship? Here is an example of authentic worship in Genesis 22:5.

"And Abraham said unto his young men, Abide ye here with the ass; and I and the lad will go yonder and WORSHIP, and come again to you."

We see here that Abraham never sang one song but his obedience to sacrifice the very thing that he wanted most demonstrated his worship of God. Think about the things you want most and cherish now. Could you lay it all down?

How does this relate to the purpose of this book?

Well, if we don't understand what truth looks like we can send up strange fire to the Lord. We have limited God's worship to merely song and dance. Although these are instruments that can assist in our worship to Him, they are not in and of themselves, worship. If we are taught what authentic worship looks like, then we can present to God what He wants from us. A life for a Life, His life for ours in obedience to Him!

Every time Abraham built an altar to God, he was showing the ultimate sacrifice of worship. Altars are often bloody messes. A place of our fleshy crucifixions but they are also places of victory.

I warn you here, that many of my written works have been considered controversial to the religious sect. I have been chosen to challenge the current church system and its theological basis for existence as we know it now.

Guess what? It's okay. Many felt this way in Jesus' time, and the hearts of man is no different today than it was back then. I am not offended, because it is my purpose. Once God begins to show and map out your destiny, your mission becomes clear.

Through trials and tribulations of life your mission is manifested. Your veil begins to fall from your eyes and a light shines way through a once darkened tunnel to a new revelation. Purpose was always there but it was overshadowed by 6 feet of dirt. Life, once lived like a body is a grave, is no longer bound by the confinement of its former tomb. Once dead we become alive!

I hope as with all my written work that you will allow the Spirit of the Lord to give you an ear to hear what the Lord is saying in this hour; that you will allow your hearts and minds to be open to receive His truth.

Remember it is the Truth we know that will set us free.

31So Jesus said to those Jews who had believed in Him, if you abide in My word [hold fast to My teachings and live in accordance with them], you are truly My disciples.32And you will know the Truth, and the Truth will set you free.
John 8:31-33

CHAPTER 1
In The Beginning!

Let me begin by relating to you the inspiration for this book.

I was on my way to my monthly professional development (PD) meeting sponsored by the school system by which I am employed.

I arrived at my professional development meeting an hour early as usual. I liked to get there early. First for the parking and secondly because it allowed me some quiet time before the day began.

As I sat in the parking lot waiting to go in, I began to listen to the musical lyrics and sounds from Maurette Brown Clark newest CD song: "One God" while eating my morning meal with a nice hot cup of coffee.

It was then that the Holy Spirit whispered softly to me,

"They keep twisting my words.

Needless to say, I thought that this must be some strong coffee, but honestly, I knew God was talking.

I stopped suddenly and turned the music down so I could be attentive and hear closely what the Spirit of the Lord was saying to me. I replied,

"Lord, I am listening!"

Again the Spirit of the Lord said,

"They keep twisting my words."

Again, I replied,

"What do you mean? I don't understand."
The Spirit of the Lord whispered again,

"They keep twisting my words."

Suddenly I felt a strong grief wash over me. I felt sick to my stomach as if I had drunk some sour milk. This feeling was God's was of sharing how he felt about this matter. Believe me it did not feel good.

And while feeling grieved, the Spirit of the Lord kept saying,

"The words! The words!"

Trying to shake off this overwhelming feeling of grief, I said,

"Lord, I do not understand but please help me to understand what you mean!"

Dead silence fell upon the vehicle once again.
As the silence penetrated the atmosphere, I listened attentively to hear what the Spirit of the Lord would say next. But only quietness continued to fill the vehicle. It felt as if Elvis had left the building, so to speak.

But just when I thought our conversation over the Spirit of the Lord whispered,

"Possess!"

While tilting my head with a puzzled look on my face, in thought, I echoed,

"Possess".

Now by this time, many thoughts began to race through my mind. I thought what a peculiar word for God to draw my attention too.

I continued to think aloud asking myself, why God would speak the word "possess". What was the significance of this word that the Spirit of the Lord wanted my attention drawn to it? Was God trying to tell me something about someone else or something about me? Was I possessed?

<u>LESSON BREAK</u>:
Let me say this before I proceed. One practice that I have come to learn is to check myself first, to clear myself of any wrong doing by turning the mirror of Gods chastisement towards me.

I know we usually do well at facing the mirror in the opposite direction, but if we really plan to grow up in Christ we must at some point turn the mirror towards ourselves.

Now let me continue…

With all sorts of thoughts racing through my head, the Holy Spirit spoke again by saying,

"The meaning! The meaning!"

Well okay, now my thoughts went into another direction. Did God want me to define its meaning? Did God want me to get others to define its meaning? What was He specifically trying to get me to see and understand about this word?

As, I have chartered this territory before, I did what I knew to do when God does this and that is NOTHING! Leave it alone until His will in this matter becomes clear.

Since the purpose wasn't clear, I meditated only on what was said. All I knew at this point was that someone twisted God's Word and the word "possess" somehow must be one of them.

Still nothing!

My final conclusion was that I was not sure what to do with this word.

Since, I tend to get over excited inwardly when this happens, I decided to try and calm my happy self-down. I began to relax my mind and just left it alone for the time being.

As I was still in my vehicle I went back to listening

to my favorite song, if only to take my mind off of this matter.

Finally, the time had come for me Togo into the building for my meeting. On my way towards the building the Lord spoke again and said,

"Ask them".

I was finally calming down and now here I was excited once again. Still not 100% clear of what was being asked of me, I replied,

"Lord, who and what am I asking them?"

LESSON BREAK:
Now you may be wondering why I am being so careful and specific. Well, I have learned along my journey that my intellect is enmity to God when it comes to trying to understand His wisdom and rightly dividing God's Word.

I have learned that true revelation, wisdom, and knowledge comes to those who are willing to empty themselves of all prior knowledge, those streams of information, beliefs, and opinions they pick up on the highway of life.

In order for use to truly understand what God is saying, we must allow God to dissect the information we previously learned from the many streams of information that have flowed from grandmothers, mama and them, moms, dads, our educational systems, friends, teachers, peers, pedagogies, and so forth. We could have a zillion degrees on our walls and a billion trophies on our desk and they still would not amount to a hill of beans when understanding
God's heart and mind.

God said, that He has chosen the foolish things of this world to confound them who think they are wise (1 Corinthian 1:27).We saw this example through the Rabbi's (teachers) in the New Testament, who possessed all knowledge of the Torah yet remained as fools knowing nothing. If they had known they would have recognized Jesus and His ministry, but they couldn't because they were blinded by their own selfish ambitions and fleshy desires for power and money. This should remind of the hearts and minds of men today!

We must let God dispose of all unnecessary thought patterns, views, and opinions that we have learned. If we keep them, we will mix it with the new wine of Gods mind, thoughts and ways

(Mark 2:22). This is how contaminated wisdom is produced even though we do not realize that it is contaminated.

Remember, God's thoughts are not our thoughts, they are higher than ours. Neither are God's ways our ways, so most of what we have learned, good and bad, must be brought under heaven's spot light for examination. (Isaiah 55:8-9)

The old wine of our thinking will contaminate what God wants to put in new and therefore contaminated thinking, produces misaligned theories and false doctrines are birthed. Therefore, a little leaven, leavens the whole lump!

"A little leaven leaveneth the whole lump.
"Galatians 5:9 Translations

One of the major areas we must contend with after we come to the altar to make confession of our guilt of disobedience and idolatrous ways towards God is to renew our mind.

Why the mind?

Well, it is the battle ground of our spiritual struggle. It is the place where Satan will fight us and keep corrupting us. Until salvation it is the area he has us in a strong hold, which is why we must renew our minds. How a man thinks, the Lord said, so is he (Proverbs 23:7).

Our thoughts are detrimental to our spiritual walk and spiritual understanding of God, His precepts and laws regarding all matters spiritual. Without the right thoughts and understanding we are an easy target for the enemy. He doesn't need to change the entire Word of God just twist it a little, put a little spin on it and there you have it, stinking thinking!

The reason why so many of us are messed up spiritually is because of the very fact that we have been bamboozled, run amuck and lied to from many of our spiritual leaders who have taught us God through tainted rose colored glass.

They have spoken to us, using phrases such as, "The Lord said and this is what the Lord means", to convince us their words are God's truth and that God is speaking to us through them. In actuality the Lord has not said what these people say nor was their meaning, his meaning.

Now, let me clarify some matters. There are many

false charlatans, wolves disguised in sheep's clothing that have used God's word to deceive and pilfer the people for selfish gain, power and reputation.

I don't want you walking away thinking that all who say these words are guilty of lying because that would not be true. God has some anointed ones who have not bowed their knees to this Baal system of church that has been erected. These people are fighting the good fight of faith and have not strayed from the straight and narrow path, but they are in the minority. Battling the wiles of the enemy on every side, listed as cast-a-ways from the many, hidden gems among the rubble, they will rise!

The enemy has spent a lot of time studying the true people of God that he has not only learned to mimic our church behaviors, and our tongues, but even our Lord's words. In order to convince us that he is one of us, the enemy has to appear as one of us, using our familiar ways to make us comfortable enough to trust in what he has sent to deceive us. If the enemy came saying, "I am lying to you", we would recognize him quickly and not trust him, so he has to appear as a sheep in wolves clothing.

This facade is not only maintained through mimicking our natural appearance and our words, but also by using God's word incorrectly, by giving it a form of godliness but lacking God's power.

It's like a Snickers bar that guarantees to satisfy your hunger but all the while it is filled with empty calories. This is why the word tells us that God's people suffer for lack of knowledge. We have been eating too much junk food!

My people are destroyed (perish, suffer) for lack of knowledge. Hosea 4:6

Why would God say this if it wasn't true? This means we are lacking truth in some things or in many things. So we are destroyed. Our destruction is spiritual. We are down trodden by the enemy because we really don't know who we are or whose we are. Thank God we are not overcome through our ignorance.

We have refused to learn, so God says, that He will refuse to let us be His priests. He says that they have forgotten the teachings of God so He will forget our children. We, as the children of God, have been too trusting of man when God has instructed us not to put our trust in no man.

Why?

The flesh of man is deceitful. In the flesh dwells no good thing especially if it is not being crucified daily and if the people are not giving themselves away to God daily. If they are not living a life pleasing to God then they can be beguiled by the enemy in any area in their life that has remained uncircumcised.

The truth of God's Word is what the enemy is after. Not your ministry, your title or church. None of that is important nor does it have any power. He wants the word of God over your life. He doesn't want you to realize your potential to know your God. If you do, you, yourself are the real threat to him not how good your voice is, your eloquent speaking styles, or how big your ministry is. Those things are superficial. The ones with the truth are fort the hardest because of the Word God has hidden in them.

Yet these are the things that the churches right now are chasing. Give me a title! I want my own ministry! I want to have a mega church! I want to have a great reputation! I want to be on TV! I want to speak to the Nation!

Paul told the Galatians in Chapter 1:6-9 that they were deserting the one who called them to live in the grace of Christ and were turning to a different gospel. Why? Because evidently there were some people throwing them into confusion and trying to pervert the Gospel of Christ.

Has the tactics of the enemy changed? NO! The enemy is still doing it today and because he has been successful in deceiving even some of the elect, God must correct this false doctrine that many have swallowed as truth.

I might be getting to this part too early, but I will just mention it for now and come back with further explanation later. Satan has planted some bad seed among the good seed; both are and have been growing up together for a long while.

Due to the lack of maturity of many saints and/or the premature germination of the good seed, some of the good seed has gotten corrupted by the bad they have grown up with. Now the good seed is corrupted and contaminated passing that same corruption and contamination on to others. You do know fungus will continue to grow unless it fumigated correctly.

It is no wonder we are confused. The sad part is that you will not feel or look confused. In fact, you will think that you are alright and that what you think or think you know is right. For example, I know many who have opened up new churches. With the need to see growth to pay bills, many have wanted their churches to grow so badly that they followed the charlatans and their devices to rape and pilfer the people.

They hooked up with crooks and began using their money, gimmicks, and growing schemes to manipulate and hurt people who are searching for answer to what ailed them. The problem is that they could not discern that they were crooks. They looked like every normal man of the cloth, so to speak.

I have heard other pastors speak with other pastors about ways to get the people to give more money, and grow their churches.

This is very popular under the babes in Christ and unfortunately there are many. Now, what constitutes a Babe? Well, it is one that remains carnal minded in thought and actions. Years of service does not constitute maturity in God.

For when the time ye ought to be teachers, ye have need that one teach you again which be the first principles of the oracles of god; and are become such as have need of milk and not of strong meat.
Hebrew 5:12

Since, they do not really know who God is or who they are; hurting and blind people put their trust and faith in a men or women who say that they do. These get people to pledge allegiance to their visions and ideals, then lock them in with rules and regulations of things that God has not told them to do, using the Word of God to do it.

This is happening everyday across the world. Christians are hurting and unfortunately they are being hurt right in the house of God by people that say God sent them, by people who say they love them.

We have been bamboozled by them. We have embraced doctrines of men, philosophies and legalism as substitutes for God's laws. However, I need to make this clear once more that this does not pertain to all of us, though to most of us it does. This poison has come through the lines of our ancestry into our blood stream. Some eat and drink religion and have no plans to change any of it. It has become a part of our thinking and has convinced us, and so what they have told us has become a way of life for us. But they were lying, and we are living a lie.

Again, back to the story...

All of a sudden it hit me. The Lord made my task clear. It was like an epiphany! God wanted to show me something. He wanted to shed light on a dark place. It was not my job to define it, at least not yet. I thought that might come down the road, but I was perfectly clear in my task now. I was to have others define the word.

God had instructed me to ask other Christians I knew and many I did not, what the word possess meant to them in relationship to Christians being possessed, which is how I derived the title of this book , and why this informational text has been written.

So with obedience, I asked everyone I encountered for several years, starting with my colleagues at the c meeting I attended that very day. On my job, in the stores, my community, in the church, and more, I asked this question...,

Can A Christian Be Possessed By An Evil Spirit?

How many that totaled, I do not know, but I can say this, when God wants to make a point, it will not take a million people to do it nor will it take countless hours upon hours researching articles, commentaries and so forth relating to a Christian being possessed to see that something is definitely wrong.

Research is not bad but should not take the place of the true Teacher, The Comforter Himself-The Holy Spirit. With just the first two people I talked to it did not take my being a rocket scientist to see the confusion that was among the people and how differently many have been taught.

After asking this question over and over again, the picture became clearer and clearer. I finally understood what God was trying to show me. It was quite ironic and sad at the same time. The different responses and views I got were as different as night and day.

I am now a witness on the earth that we are confused. I heard and witnessed it for myself.

CHAPTER 2
DATA ANALYSIS

As a result of my mission and assignment, I quickly discovered that many had different interpretations of what the word "possess" meant in relationship to a Christian being possessed by evil spirits, but many agreed on definition of the word "possess", and that was "to control".

Now you might ask the questions, how can this be? If we claim to serve the one and only true living God, how can we all have so many interpretations of a matter?

Well, for sure we cannot say the problem is with God. There is only one God, Right? One Holy Spirit! Right! Then using the process of elimination, it is US!

Jesus left the Holy Spirit, our Comforter and Teacher to those who accept Christ through Salvation, the one that guides and leads us into all truths concerning God's Word. So how can we all be so far off from the truth?

Well, I do have some understanding of how this miscommunication between man and God happens. God has dealt with me for many years about this matter and part of the problem has been discussed prior in the text. This issue will also be further elaborated later in this book.

Now based upon this type of confusion, it would make anyone wonder if God could be senile. Or, does He know what He is talking about?

GOD FORBIDS! It is not God, but us.

Certainly not! Indeed, let God be true, but every man a liar. As it is written: "That You may be justified in Your words, And may overcome when You are Judged...Romans 3:4"

Sad to say, it is us. We have changed things (words, scripture, etc.) to fit our own purpose. This is nothing new. The Pharisees and the Scribes did the same thing in the time of Jesus. They knew the Laws of Moses, and the Torah. They read the laws and the books of the prophet every Sabbath. They were advent scholars of His word. If there were theology schools then, they would have been the graduates and then teachers of it, but instead they had synagogues. They knew these prophecies better than anyone else yet they lacked wisdom, revelation, and understanding of the knowledge that they claimed to know.

God trusted these religious men to teach His people about Him. How they are to live and what was pleasing and unpleasing to Him.

Instead they added yeast! The question to ask is…..

Why?

CHAPTER 3
A Ball of Confusion

We left off with the question of WHY?

Well, let's look at Matthew 23: (*The Scribes were officials in the temple.*) Jesus now spoke for the last time in public. He had more to say to his disciples in private, but he now left the temple for the last time.

Let's stop here for a minute!

Notice that although Jesus spoke in the temple, he did not tell them everything. There were some hidden things that were to be shared only with his disciples.

Notice again that the Scribes were not looked upon as disciples even though they were the keepers of the Laws of Moses and the Torah. Even though they spoke in the synagogues every Sabbath, they were not disciples. You ever wonder why? Why didn't Jesus choose these learned men as disciples instead of the most unlikely fisherman to be His chosen disciples? I will let you chew on that for a while.

The scribes were not teachable men! They thought they knew it all. So when Jesus came on the scene he showed them up and they did not like it one bit. I believe it is because of the motives of their hearts and what they did with the Word of God that eliminated them from this consideration.

Let me prophetically speak to them who are looked down upon and considered to be the "least" among them who think they are great. God said, *"You don't have no titles, or prestigious position in the church; you just love God and want to do His will. You are often unrecognized by man but God sees you foremost. God said, "You shall be first!" Many of you will be candidates of Gods supernatural power. Many will try to figure out the how and why but it will be you that God will use to confound them who think they are wise."* SELAH!

Now let us get back...

Jesus was very patient with those who disagreed with him. He listened to all their questions although they tried to make him give wrong answers. He understood what their questions meant. He answered them perfectly.

Let me stop again!

We see here that the scribes did not agree with Jesus. What this says is that God's truth is not going to agree with our current day theologians either. Like the scribes, they are no longer teachable because they have this "God like understanding" down pack. You won't be able to teach them anything. They have their degrees with PhD. and Doctor stamped to their
names and they feel that they have arrived.

What can a little nobody like her teach me they say? She isn't like us. She doesn't fit with us. She has no credentials nor has she graduated from the best universities. Isn't this what they saw in Jesus, A carpenter's son from Nazareth? They asked, "Can anything good come out of Nazareth?"

Yes it did, but they were blinded by their own images and too vain to see it much like those leaders present today. Some of the most anointed people aren't in the pulpit; they are in pews, still in jails, on corners and more! So don't count out people or dispel them as nothing because the very person you discount could be the very one that has God's healing in their hands to save your life!

I do not like talking about myself but for the sake

of this book I have been instructed that I must. Chosen to be one of them by God to correct wrong thinking, I have been persecuted by many who say they love God and can discern His Spirit.

God has often called me a John the Baptist in regard to the call on my life. When he commissioned me to go forth I was left with this charge-"Set My House In Order!"

Of course, I do not claim to know it all but if you listen to some of the people who think they know me, they will tell you a different story. They will say, I think I know it all when in actuality I do not think this at all. You will never make me guilty in that area. If I thought that way then I would be just as guilty as the Rabbis (teachers) in Jesus' time were and like those of today.

With that charge, came persecution beyond your wildest beliefs. I, through God, became the voice of one crying out in the wilderness, make ye straight the way of the Lord. With every word I spoke came disagreement and cynicism. Like Jesus I was faced with them who disagreed with me, who did not know what they had among them.

True story!

I once had to face a couple who I had been friends with for well over twelve years. In the course of this time I had shared with them many prophecies and visions that God had shared with me. These golden nuggets as I often refer to such prophesy as pertained to mankind, the world and revelation of God's word. Some of these things pertained to future and the present events as well.

Of course, when I shared these things with them, they appeared to listen with attentive ears. Never in my wildest dreams would I have ever thought what God revealed they felt about me.

Do you know all that time as they listened they did not believe that God was speaking through me?

Imagine that right! I guess they must have thought it was my imagination, a bad meal, or something. When God told me this, I was in complete shock over the matter.

I mean I shared some deep stuff. Many of the golden nuggets that I shared we are experiencing right now in this county. I could not believe it. They would even Amen these things, and more. Clueless, yes I was, because I wasn't looking for evil. I trusted them and knew they trusted me. We spent days and hours in fellowship with one another sharing God's Word, prayer and interceding with and for one another.

One day I had to confront the couple's wife on another serious matter. God had said that although they thought that I really loved God they felt that I was too "over the top", zealous, and out there for them.

So I became a mission for them to accomplish. The couple's wife had set out to change me. To mirror me into her version of a Godly Woman!

<u>LESSON BREAK:</u>
People of God stop trying to fit everyone into this common mold that the church world has created. Many great people were great because they were unique not because they were common.

Like the nature of the world you turn up your noses at anything different. You reject the unfamiliar and because of it you have rejected many blessings and answers to your prayers. It was not that God had not sent or answered them it is because you could not recognize his answer. So this loss is yours.

Do you realize that this is exactly what they did to Jesus? They did not see God instead they looked at where Jesus grew up, what kind of job Joseph held, and probably his outfit. They judged Him falsely by external means in the same way we continue to do today.

God once said that many of us would have even rejected John the Baptist because he did not come to your church edifices with the proper attire.

Is that true?

Search your hearts to see if it could be!

Let's get back now….

Believe me I was nobody's project but to make a long story short, it was some years later before that same couple's wife would come and say these words to me.

COUPLE'S WIFE: (phone rings) *Hello Prophetess, you busy?*

ME: *No, what's going on? Long time no hear.*

COUPLE'S WIFE: *I wanted to know if I could stop by and speak with you.*

ME: *SURE, Is there something wrong?*

COUPLE'S WIFE: *No, nothing is wrong. My Husband and I were up last night talking about what God showed each of us concerning you.*

ME: *Okay come on by.*
(Well you know that aroused my curiosity immediately.)

(The arrival of the Couple's wife)
ME: *Hey what's up Pastor? Have a seat. So, what's going on now!*

COUPLE WIFE: *My husband and I were talking and reminiscing on old times. He had wondered how you were doing and asked if I had spoken with you lately.*

ME: *Yeah we had some good times.*

COUPLE'S WIFE: *Yes we did! While reminiscing, God showed us that all that time you were with us that you were sharing the heart and mind of God with us; those secret things not given to all.*

ME: *(Nodding with shock) Wow!*

COUPLE'S WIFE: God said, that we did not know what we had in front of us and so we repented to God for not appreciating the gift He gave us through you and for the things he was allowing you to share with us. We wanted to let you know we are so sorry.

I was speechless! I was also honored at the same time. Most people won't come back and admit their wrong that took a lot of humility from them to be obedient.

I shared this to tell you that even among the many that we associate with as friends; many will question and disagree with the very things that God has shared with you. This was also to show the likeness of my situation among the present day leaders to the ones in the time of Jesus. These were not people who recently got saved, they were veterans. They were Pastors of a church. People who knew the Lord

They were people who loved Jesus but had a view of God in a certain way that when the truths I shared with them were revealed, they rejected it just like the Rabbi's did to Jesus in the synagogues when he spoke. Just like the Scribes and

Pharisees could not recognize Jesus; my friends could not recognize me.
.

Back to Matthew 23.

Jesus just listened understanding the motives of their questions. They wanted to trip him up. Get Him to say things wrong to find him guilty, like they do now, but He answered them perfectly.

We will have to be prayed up and know who we are when God sends us to them. These people will have their guns loaded with their doctrinal truths ready to fire at will. They will be ready to attack what you say in a coy way and try to trip you up too. They will try to prove you wrong to claim you false, but what they won't see is the backing confirmation of God as they did not see in the time of Jesus.

This is a perfect example to those who are called like myself to correct the wrong thinking and misaligned Word of God in the Houses of the Lord. Always deal with them in gentleness, temperance, and great understanding.

When you come against people's customs you are

basically telling them that they have been wrong all this time and it upsets their world. That's what Jesus was doing, changing the order, practices, and the thoughts which overshadowed the religious men and their reputations.

To some of us, the reputations we have built are all we have. If you remove one stone from our built monument, the whole thing can tumble down and that is scary for many.

It was for me.

God had to breakdown my belief system and tear up anything that I understood that was not even close to what He thought. So I do understand how they feel. My question to you is how long will you continue to resist the Lord's ways?

Back to Matthew 23

Like Jesus, He was humble and patient. Many people must have admired this. But the time had now come when Jesus would speak out clearly. It was very important that the crowds of people understood Jesus.

Let me stop again!

When people disagree with us it becomes important that we act appropriately and not unseemly. I have learned just to smile at them with the understanding that they are sick with deception and that they lack true discernment to see and hear the difference.

However, there will come a time when God will speak clearly, as His Word must be understood. He will use whoever and He won't care about our feelings or our so called order of right and wrong.

We, the church, have really stumbled over this matter. The enemy, through his lying servants has made us to feel that if we speak up and out, we are out of order. Now this is a topic that needs to be addressed but not in this book, perhaps in another one.

However this is done especially with Prophets! They have silenced many of the true ones by raising false ones in their place. The question is whose order are we following? This order that we have established is built around false doctrine and ideologies of men, not the God sent ones but those who positioned and sent themselves.

There will come a time when we are chosen for

such a task, will be unable to hold our peace. God does not want us to fear what man will do to us because the Lord promises to fight our battles and confirm them who He sends.

Now I am not giving a license for every renegade spirit to go into the houses of God to say, the Lord said and the only voices they hear are from Mickey Mouse and Donald Duck. The backing of the Lord comes when He has willed a matter. You have no right to correct anything that God has not willed for correction and should only be corrected at set time given by Him and for Him.

Nor does it mean that if God does send one of His chosen ones to your church that He needs your permission. I know we have adopted the philosophy that the pastor has the only authority, but this is not true! The entire Five Fold ministry has authority but we haven't grown up this way, so we follow another doctrine of order set by Catholicism.

Like I said, I won't get into that much as that subject is best suited to another book.

I never quite understood this but if the church you have belongs to God then He decides what is to be done, right! Does God have to get man's approval too? Does one man make this decision alone or in the counsel of many? Who are the many? Who chooses the many? It should start with the Apostle. The pastor is not even in the first ranking of God's order; it's the Apostle then the prophet.

Many claim that their church belongs to God yet God does not have any real authority in such a church. The authority is in name only, not in submission. We are saying God does but only if God is doing what we want to do and saying what we want to hear. We like the emotionalism of slaying people in the spirit, shouting, yelling or the word of blessing and promises on the house by the prophets. We like that kind of Fluff. What if God himself comes with correction or rebuke? Would the deliverer of that correction or rebuke be allowed to speak?

HUM!

I do not need to tell you the response to that because you and I both know what the response will be. It is in our nature to control or dominate. It is that natural desire to control that gets in the way of what God bids to do. It becomes about us, our church, and ministries.

We hide our true motives under scripture by manipulating it to keeps it sounding spiritual. However, we can't fool God nor them who God has chosen to show this too. The time is coming that the permission we once thought we needed from man will come from God and the control nuts are not going to like it!

Now back to the rest of Matthew 23!

The Pharisees and Scribes seemed to behave well. They prayed often in public. They gave away a 10th part of what they had. They even gave away a 10th of all kinds of small vegetables. They knew and could repeat much of the Law. Many people thought that these men were 'very holy'. But their behavior was in fact the opposite of all that Jesus taught. Jesus had to make people understand this.

Having a form of Godliness but denying the power thereof...2 Timothy 3:5

Jesus said that the Pharisees taught many good things. They taught God's law. But the important thing was to obey it. Jesus called the Pharisees 'graves that men have painted white' (*Matthew 23:27*). They looked good and holy on the outside.

In fact, their lives were selfish and greedy. They showed this by the way that they behaved with Jesus. They will show it by the way they behave towards me. They wanted people to praise them. They wanted to have the best seats at meetings. 'Do the things that they teach', Jesus said, 'But do not do the things that they do'.

Some things were not important. But the Pharisees said that these things were important. For example, they said that it was important to give away a 10th of some plants. They did not think much about how people behaved to one another. They did not think about being kind or fair to other people. They did not like what Jesus taught. This stopped some people from trusting Jesus. Jesus spoke out about the Pharisees and the Scribes very strongly.

This is our modern day churches guilt too. We have made the least important practices of church more important (anniversaries, programs, festivities, etc.) than the important purpose of church, which is to build character in people, integrity, relationship with God, spiritual warfare, and more.

Even now, many who claim that they are hearing

from God aren't truly hearing from God at all. They have us paying our tithes to build monuments of nothingness and statues unto themselves but not correctly instructing us in the teachings of God. They are more concerned about the superficial things of this world than building us to manifest Christ like images. We are the building that must be built eradicated, not the ones of stone, brick and mortar.

Instead they say, Let us have fun! Let us have a good time in the Lord! So this is now what we come to look for, a good time. They focus on our emotionalism. They confused emotionalism with spiritualism and thus we think that what we are experiencing is God's Spirit. Should church have exciting things to do? Sure it can, but what is exciting? The first question to ask you is to answer this, what did God create church for?

Once this question is answered, we must ask, what have we turned it into? It was created for our instruction and prayer; a gathering place where we could come on one accord and learn about God, His ways and His thoughts and pray.

Instead we have made it an entertainment center.

You enter in and the program is written and performed for us. There is nothing sacred about the altar of God we resurrected. The Sanctuary we call it. We have made God's house of prayer a den of thieves. We have elected to accept less performances of God's Spirit than we do the performances of man's talent.

We have been trained like monkeys to perform tasks irrelevant to the Will of God. God is not against us living life, just against living a life unrighteous and predicated by lies , as opposed to living Godly truths.

Granted, all leaders are hearing voices; Lord knows that there are many in the land, but whose voice are they hearing? God has One Voice and it should echo the same to all that hear Him. God may choose different analogies or different ways of presenting things, but the meaning or outcome of what He is trying to tell us should and will be the same. A little deeper, a little richer but the underlining message should be different. Finally it must produce. Now we can produce things by our hands and work darn hard at it, but when God does it, you won't break a sweat.

My sheep hear my voice, and I know them, and they

follow me: John 10:27

We should be able to go to another city, state, country and find agreement among those that are serving the True and Living God, speaking the same things, but many are not.

Even within in the same cities and towns people are speaking different things. We should be of one accord. We should not have mixed messages, but we have them. We can't even go from one denomination to another denomination within our own cities and speak of one accord. We find ourselves divided on many issues. Something is wrong and the problem is not with God, but with us.

Now before you get all willy-nilly, there are two types of agreements, a righteous one that result in Liberty to the captives and religious ones which resulting Legalism. Do you realize that misconceptions can find agreements with misconceptions? Two cannot walk together unless they agree. Wrong can find agreement among the wrong and right among the right!

That is what we clearly saw between Jesus and the

Scribes, Liberty verse Legalism. It still occurs today! Jesus wants to liberate us not keep us bound.

With the Charismatic movement it made it easy to link up with only those who believe like you believe. Where with the other doctrinal religions they have a set of procedures and rules and all must follow it. The Charismatic movement had much good in it and much that was disorderly and destructive in it as well. God used them but they are not at all the order of God. They rejected the Scriptural order and took part of the revelation. Many ran who were not sent, causing confusion.

I know that what I am about to say is going to disturb and upset the religious sect, but denominations are of the devil. That's right I said it, so please take the daggers out of my back and stop giving me evil looks. We put too much value on these man-made procedures, rules, philosophies, and interpretations that have only a form of Godliness attached to it, but no power.

Each division did their part in holding us down spiritually, but we have to be prepared to move past the falsehoods and deceits in them to align ourselves to God's Word.

However, I will tell you my reasoning in this belief. It is because denominations cause divisions. When the Apostles went through the cities on their assignments, setting up churches for Christ, they spoke unified on one message concerning Salvation. The Gospels are four books that highlight the life, walk and teachings of our
Lord & Savior Jesus Christ and even though what each saw and experienced may have been different, the message did not change.

The New Testament was written to keep everyone on one accord and to teach us about Christian living, what God expected from us, and what to be aware of. The message has not changed nor has God's desires to have a unified body, but somehow we have managed to find different interpretations of these messages preached across the pulpits worldwide.

How can this be?

The Word of the Lord tells us that any kingdom divided against itself cannot stand (Matthew 12:25). God is not about division, but multiplication. Satan divides to conquer. The only thing He asked us to separate is ourselves from the world and we aren't doing a good job at that. For that fact, we are looking more and more like the world as the days and years go by.

This division opened up the pores of our skin and allowed bacteria to creep into our blood stream. We became infected by the false ideologies, doctrines of and traditions of men! We need a spiritual transfusion! There are those who want to stop the transfusion from taking place by using lies against God' true anointed one. They were born with the anecdote we need. We need to truth!

No wonder we are screwed up! We are filled with leaven and it does not take a lot of leaven to spoil the whole leaf. Until we allow God to get rid of the leaven we have in our church system, we will always serve God's Word, teach God's Word, preach God's Word, and interpret God's word with distortions in it. This leaven will defile the very Word of God, and the people who hear it.

The devil knows that. He also knows the power behind the truth of God's Word. He set in order a plan to sabotage the church by planting bad seed among the good seed. To confuse us and get us off the trail of knowing the truth. That is why God says, *"If you hold to my teachings, you are my disciples. Then you will know the truth and the truth will set you free* (John8:31-32)."

As a church body we are guilty because we have not held fast to God's teaching. We need the truth because as a church we are fooled, by the falsehoods, misrepresentations, and lies that were sold to us as truth.

The Lord remains us on this matter in 1 Corinthian 1:27, *"But God hath chosen the foolish things of this world to confound the wise; and God hath chosen the weak things of the world to confound the things that are strong."* Even the Pharisees and the religious men of that day could not understand Jesus even though they knew the law. Doctrines and fables of Men will do just that, pollute the Word of God.

I do not expect everyone who reads this either to understand although I hope that they would. I know that this message will collide and bump heads with many because of how they have been taught. I am not here to fight them, but to liberate them. Help them free themselves from themselves. Bring them to repentance for not truly seeking God, but trusting in man.

I speak to you the truth in love with hope that you run on to victory the race Christ has set before you.
SELAH

CHAPTER 4
DATA ANALYSIS

I love God's people but some of God's blessed children are so full of the devil's misconceptions that they can barely tell you their name, much more interpret God's Word. Now that may seem a little harsh to some and it very well may be, but it is time for us to stop sparing the rod of God. We have done that by ignoring sin and allowing anything to go on in the house of God because we don't want to offend people.

God is the only interpreter of His Word and the Holy Spirit is the designated one to help us interpret it. Many of us try to use degrees of education or logical reasoning to interpret God's Word. Let me tell you such actions will miss the mark every time. Only God knows what He means in every word that is written in black on white paper.

Speaking of black and white, the Holy Spirit enlightened me to this very important fact about reading and interpreting God's Word. He said; don't just read what is written in black ink but the white also. Now I will say that puzzled me for a while because there are no words written in white, but he wasn't talking about words written in white. He was saying that while each word is written with black ink on white paper, it is about the white between each letter and word that isn't said that he wants me to focus on.

We read between the lines and only the Holy Spirit can help us see and understand what is not written or the unobvious.

God's Rhema is not released to just anyone. As with everything that God gives us, we must first be tested and tried and found faithful, loyal and trustworthy in His sight. If He tells us not to cast our pearls among swine, do you really believe that He would cast His golden nuggets of His own Word among swine?

"Give not that which is holy unto the dogs, neither cat ye your pearls before swine, lest they trample them under their feet and turn again and rend you."
Matthew 7:8

We were all swine until we came unto repentance before God. God's Word is everything to Him. He said that Heaven and earth will pass away first, but

His Word! His Word, His Word shall remain! God is not going to let us have what is most precious to Him until we have earned it.

The wise he will confound as well as them who think they are strong. You must come like sheep and sheep are not intelligent animals but they can distinguish their master's voice from among any other.

Now granted, the Bible is given to us all and that is God's word in logos form but Rhema is another form that is not easily gotten by many. That wisdom he shares with whom he chooses. I know many claim to have God's gift, but we as a body need to be extra careful and more discerning of man.

Now, many people who gathered around Jesus heard Him speak, but were clueless to what He said. The learned religious men did not understand what He was saying either. So I will say what Jesus has said many times before, let them that have an ear to hear, hear what the Spirit of the Lord is saying.

Let me continue....

After talking with people and sharing in their understanding of the word "possess" in relationship to evil spirits, the task was complete and my understanding was enlightened as to what God's grievances were about. God had every right to feel the way He did. We have messed up and we have gotten away from the truth.

This not about the word possess. Possess is just one of many words that we used incorrectly in context of God's meaning of it. Wherever there is confusion beware the enemy is in the midst of it. He has been doing and believing things for so long we don't even challenge it anymore.

God instructed me to dig even further. This is what leads me into the making of this pamphlet. I am well aware that many have written on this topic and I proposed this same point to God. I was told by His Majesty, Jesus Christ, that what I am instructed to write will not be the same, but will piggy back and confirm only what He himself has been talking, sharing, with others on this matter.

I thank God for all of the pastors, evangelist and teachers, who have been in the forefront of this battle, but there have been two silent voices in the fivefold ministry and they are the voices of the Apostle and the Prophet.

Led by Jezebel, many have tried to do away with them, but they are returning, not that they ever were ever gone. The most crucial one for hearing the heart and mind of God is the voice of the Prophet and this in no way undermines any of my fivefold brethren. However it needs to be clarified that the prophet's role is crucial for direction and clarity of God Words. Each of us have our part but we need each other to survive.

Now understand two things, 1. Prophecy is different from the Prophet and 2. Many false prophets from Jezebel have gone through out the land mimicking the real prophets. Dark spirits have lead many astray and have succeeded with their deceptions and lies. God knows that many of His children are being destroyed because of lack of knowledge, but God's loves us to much to leave us ignorant unless we choose to be.

It's A New Season! A Season of New Revelation and Manifestation of His True Power.
Selah!

Due to the contamination among many of us so-called mature Saint of God, God is raising a generation that will speak His wisdom, bring correction and order to the confusion, and obey His will.

This generation is often called the remnant. We are the ones spoken in Revelations12:17 that the enemy will make war against. Satan will come against the remnant church with everything and anyone he can use.

Why?

Because we are the ones which have keep Gods commandments and have the testimony of Jesus Christ.

Unfortunately, it grieves me to say that Satan has used Christians against other Christians to do this and has been successful over the centuries that we find that what is popular is not always truth and what is truth is not always popular.

This remnant church represents a transition in the command of the old system to the new system right before God's return. God once showed me a church rising out of the church. That He had hidden in this present corrupt church system a people who will do His will the way He willed it to be. See the next generation has nothing to do with age, religion, origin, doctrines, but with spiritual destiny. They have been chosen. Some are here and establishing them now to receive the harvest from the churches God will close one way or another.

God knew the state that the church would be in and how the guards of the former generation would become beguiled by Jezebel who called herself a prophet but is self-appointed; that they would fall into the trap of the enemy to seek power, money, and fame. That is why so many are claiming themselves to be prophets/prophetess and Apostle. Like a new wave or a new fad, many are trying to get themselves self-appointed to a position that is not supposed to be appointed by men but by God.

In these high ranking positions they have the ability to damage God's people and this is not a new strategy because they have been doing this for a long time. The stakes are higher now and time for the enemy is drawing near. Why do you think we have so many position hungry people? They want power, money and fame that is why!

The time of the apostle and prophet is here and so many now must strategically get into these positions to continue what they started years ago. If it sounds like a war, it is! This is a war between the Kingdom of God and the Kingdom of darkness and we are theorize.

The Kingdom of God suffers (allows) violence but the violent (aggressive) must take it by force
Matthew 11:12

This is a spiritual war, a war that many of us were not trained to fight because we were so busy having church, we weren't being preparing to become it. We must become violent (aggressive) and relentless in our strategies against our adversary. We must wake up out of our sleep and slumber. We must assume our position in the earth. It is up to us! God is not going to do it for us! It's time to walk as God!

Like Jeremiah, God knew who they would be since the foundation of the world. So I hear you say, what has all of this to do with whether or not a Christian can be possessed by an Evil Spirit?

But oh! It must definitely does.

The one who teaches us helps steers and develops our spiritual understand of God and what He means. Who plants seed in our vineyard most definitely impacts our spiritual growth, spiritual understanding and our spiritual relationship with God.

I need it to be perfectly clear on the purpose and intention of this specific written work. I am not here to debate over ideologies or convince you if one can or cannot be possessed by an evil spirit. You will make that decision even after reading this book. What we decide as truth does not change one bit of God's truth. However it leaves us ignorant and as God said "My people are destroyed for lack of knowledge (Hosea 4:6)".

I am writing to inform of procedural infractions and errors that have been formulated through many forms of doctrine because of the misinterpretation of words and their meanings that in the long run has affected our perception and understanding of God.

Again, this is why God states that many ought to be

teacher but need to go back to receive the elementary teaching again because some where their foundation of thinking and their understanding is faulty.

Truly, I am just setting the stage.

CHAPTER 5
A Tale of Two Cities

I was recently asked by my oldest brother, and it is pretty ironic too, if I was possessed?

I laughed so hard because this question was in perfect timing and relevance to this topic. When God has you to talk on a matter, it amazes me how He sets and lines you up for the experience.

I was asked this question because my brother felt that I was going too far with this "religion thing" as he called it. My brother who claims he to be a student and brother of the Muslim faith wanted to cause nothing but confusion.

That's what the enemy wants to do and he doesn't care how or through whom it is done. He will use whatever means necessary to accomplish his task. He does this when he want to manipulate you into his own point of view.

I did not take my brothers question as an insult, but as a compliment. Sometimes we take to heart what people say about us, and to us. We need to get over some things and stop allowing the enemy to "get our goat" so to speak. "Get your goat" is an idiom or another way of saying that we let people annoy us to the point that we get mad and upset.

When we are doing it God's way, insults wills come. But how you perceive those insults can and will result in one of two things. One, it can result in you getting mad and losing your temper. Two, it can result in you looking at it as a compliment which is how I took my brothers question of me being possessed.

My answer to him was,

"I sure am."

He grew quiet on the spot. It was almost like he expected me to fight him over what he said or be insulted by it.

Probably, if I had not done the research of this word or if God had not been dealing with me regarding it, I might have been insulted but it was like I was prepared for this attack. So, what I told him was this.

LESSON BREAK

It is a good thing when we can reflect those fiery darts that the enemy throws at us with our shield of faith. The shield of faith not only defends our whole body but is also our armor. It keeps the darts of the enemy from our chest, waist, arms and legs. No wonder the Bible says we should have it above all.

The shield of faith has a specific function which the Bible makes abundantly clear; quench all the fiery darts of the enemy or wicked one. Not some of them but all.

A shield moved with each attack. A skilled soldier can use a shield to hold back the darts of the enemy no matter where they come from. But many of us don't use our shields often. Most of us have them leaning against the wall, collecting dust.

Instead of using our shield, we fight fire with fire. In other words we trade insults with our attackers. We jab at them as they are jabbing at us using their methods which are not Godly in their intent.

Now back to the story!

I told him that not only am I possessed, but that I wanted God to possess every part of my mind, body, and soul. I want His ways to be my ways, His thoughts to be my thoughts. I want Him to truly pilot what remains of my life here on earth; Full and complete control of every thought, every move, and every action.

His response was one puzzling to him that he said one day you can introduce me to this God you serve that I might know Him in this way!

Now that might seem to be a little "extreme" for most and that is okay. I figured that since I screwed up most of my life following my own way anyhow, what could I lose by turning my life over to its creator.

Sometimes "extreme" but I would like to choose the word "radical" is what we have to be for the enemy because he doesn't believe we mean what we say anyhow. But look at the results when I chose to use my shield.

This was my defining moment, an experience that helped me to further understand the use of this word in a different light. Not seeing it as evil things, but as a good thing. So possession for me at that moment took on the meaning of control or take over, but I have discovered that this word has more than one meaning which led me further into my next task, that of defining what the term POSSESS (ED) meant.

Let me make note that although I am using reference materials to gain some understanding, it does not provide the full true meaning of what God is trying to say. God is the author of His truth and the Holy Spirit is the ultimate revealer of such truth. What is offered here is a snippet, a fraction of what was learned along with the countless hours, months and years of laying before God for His truth which cannot fit into this single manuscript. All that I learned was placed on the altar of God for understanding, His understanding. Not me combining my intellect with His or assuming what He means either. Like Jesus, I emptied myself for the mind of God.

Chapter 6
Defining the Moment

Based upon my research of this term, I discovered that possess also meant, to have, to influence, to own, to control. So I looked little deeper and discover that the term "own" also meant to control and to have. As I explored more and more of each words definition, I found that they had similar meanings.

Let's look at the meaning of "possess" according to Merriam Webster Collegiate Dictionary 19th ED.

Possess /ed/ion 1a: To have or hold as property; OWN b: to have as an attribute, knowledge or skill 2a: to take into one's possession b: to enter into and control firmly: DOMINATE ***c: to bring or cause to fall under the influence, possession, or control of some emotional intellectual reaction;*** 3a: to state as owner b: to make the owner holder- used in passive construction to indicate simple possession. ***4. Influenced or controlled by something (as an evil spirit or a passion).*** 5a. The act of having or taking into control. B. control or occupancy of property without regard to ownership c: ownership 6: something owned, occupied or controlled; PROPERTY **7a: domination by something (as evil spirits, a passion, or an idea)** b: a psychological state in which an individual's normal personality is replaced by another c: the fact or condition of being self-controlled.

WOW! Now that is a lot. Notice that it is very repetitive in its meanings. You constantly see the words: control, influence, have, property, and dominate, but that word "control" really stood out.

I took the liberty of highlighting definitions 2c, 4 and 7a because they were relevant to this topic of study.

Now let's look at a Holman's Bible dictionary's meaning of DEMON POSSESSION Holman's: The ***control*** of an individual's personality so that actions are ***influenced*** by an evil demonic spirit.

You can see here that both "*control*" and "influence" are used in its definition. So let us define them now.

1. **Influence**-to flow in. from in, power, authority; the capacity to have an effect on the character,

development or behavior of someone of something, or the effect itself. 1a. the ethereal fluid held to flow from the starts and to effect the actions of human b: an emanation of occult power held to derive from stars. 2. An emanation of spiritual or moral force 3a.the act of power of producing an effect without apparent exertion of force or direct exercise of command b. corrupt interference.

2. **Control** /ken'trol/ 1. The power to *influence* or direct people's behavior or course of events. 2. To have power over, power or authority to guide or manage.

As you can read many of these words are interchangeable with one another and take on similar if not exact meanings of the other.

Now let us take a look at one more word "Dominate".

3. Dominate: /da-me-nat/ 1: Rule, Control<an empire that dominated the world> 2: to exert the supreme determining or guiding *influence* on.

I know you are tired of reading definition but it is

important to know how each word relates one to another; in all our getting God commands that we get understanding.

To relate that word to the Bible in regard to possession, most of those described as demon-possessed in the New Testament are adult men, but certain women were also delivered from the influence of evil spirits.

Luke 8:2- And certain women which had been healed of evil spirits and infirmities, Mary call Magdalene out of whom went seven devils.

Luke 13:11- And behold there was a woman who had a spirit of infirmity eighteen years and was bent over and could in no way raise herself up.

Luke 13:16- So ought this woman, being a daughter of Abraham, whom Satan has bound- think of it- for eighteen years, be loosed from this bond on the Sabbath?

The signs of demon possession in the New Testament include: speechlessness (Matthew 9:33); deafness (Mark 9:25); blindness (Matthew 12:22); fierceness (Matthew 8:28); unusual strength (Mark 5:4); convulsions (Mark 1:26); and foaming at the mouth (Luke 9:39).

In my experience, I have seen many people in the come to the altar for deliverance. Upon the laying of hands from the elders of the church, individuals saved and unsaved alike, have been known to convulse, foam at the mouth, vomit and more and I am not talking about unsaved individuals either, saved ones too!

Most of the New Testament references to demon possession appear in the Gospels and represent the outburst of satanic opposition to God's work in Christ.

I love how such references define demon possession as a control of one's personality. With this it suggests that we need to also look at what the enemy seeks to control. Our personality is the particular combination of emotional, attitudinal, and behavioral response patterns of an individual. Each of these is an influence of our actions. I guess we can now say that the demonic forces desire to gain access to the fleshy parts of us not yet under total influence or possession of the Spirit of God. The more we yield and learn of

God's ways, and adjust ourselves to them, we become more like Christ. So what does it suggest when we go to the altar, confess our sins, and don't yield? A BIGGER STRUGGLE!

We will always contend for the faith. This battle is daily and continuous. We will wrestle with evil forces for a majority of the time we are on earth. However, our personality is a major strategic factor in the demonic forces plan to gain control of saved Christians. This plan is not just to control where our souls go, (though that is the ultimate plan), but to control life here on earth by making us turn from God. If this were not true, we would not be right now experiencing such a great fall away from the body of Christ. We would not have so many contenders of the faith being led away by seducing spirits. This should suggest once again that as Christians we must be transformed by the renewing of our mind daily. As a man thinks so he is, and thus if the thinking of the man is warped, it defiles the man and leaves him/her open for spiritual opposition, influences, possessions and more!

Does this still happen today? Do demons still have outburst of satanic opposition to God's work in

Christ? We can see that through the world clearly this is the case, but that's not our problem. Our problem is that we can't see it in our own saved folk, so to speak.

To see it, we must first define satanic opposition to God's work in Christ.

CHAPTER 7
POSSESSION VS OPPRESSION

Demonic oppression and possession are two distinct types of demonic interactions, though both cause harassment and influence over a person.

Possession is a state in which the demon gains full command of a person's body. The demon takes away the person's ability to use their physical body, will, consciousness and freedom. A person adopts the personality, voice, and actions of the demon by housing the body of the person.

Oppression on the other hand is an indirect attack wherein a person's behavior and entire life is influenced by the demon but the person retains control over their physical body and mind.

Now let me stop right here because I want us to focus on one important factor in this understanding that the Holy Spirit brought to my attention. The only factor separating oppression from possession is the maintaining control over one's physical body and mind. God showed me that one of the requirements, commandments of a

Christian is the renewal of the mind. If this is true and it is, then why renew the mind if we are saved and converted through repentance?

God has showed me though the Holy Spirit that our mind is still under the control of its former slave master. Everything that we have learned and accepted as our views of life has been influenced. Our will, freedom and actions of our physical body are all in some way controlled. The concepts and views we have are formatted and developed by a corrupted system. There would be no need to renew if the mind we came in with wasn't corrupted. We are supposed to gain the same mind that was also in Christ Jesus. Which means that we must allow God though the Holy Spirit to get rid of and change our thoughts, views, philosophies and so forth.

Possession now takes on a broader view. It is not exclusive to just our physical body but our mind too. If possession include losing control over our mind then we entered into salvation already messed up and with a lack of control over our mind with the hope that if we yield our mind to Christ and allow Him to really renew our mind to one that truly thinks like Christ.

The Word tells us in Proverbs 23:7..."*that as a man thinks in his heart, so is he*". The heart is the place where all the issues of life flow from and has been proven to be quite deceitful. In the heart man harbors all sought of evil things and the heart and mind work together. God call man's heart evil because as Matthew 15:19 states *"For out of the heart comes evil thoughts-murder, adultery, sexual immorality, theft, false testimony, slander."*

According to Jeremiah 17:9, the heart is so deceitful above all things and beyond cure because man's heart is incapable of seeing things in a straightforward manner.

Corrupt thinking leaves a man defiled with corruption, and wrong thinking makes him wrong. This is why the enemy wages war against our mind. It is a place where we can be held hostage, place in chains, and fettered in bondage.

Now I know you may be wondering, "Where is she going with this?" Well I am laying yet another foundation for truth, a new truth to many, and for a few confirmation of a truth they have already discovered.

The mind is a vital part of our walk with Christ.

The mind has been known to be the battlefield of the enemy; the place he seeks to grab a hold of, but the question is, why?

Why is the mind so important to the enemy? It is important because the mind is the driving force of what we do, think and say. If Satan can get us to believe lies and untruths then he can deceive us and keep us from true freedom and power in Christ. It allows him greater access of control over us.

Well opposition starts the moment you decide to follow Jesus. Another way of looking at opposition is through the word persecution. Opposition is not always the result of consequences to wrong things you have done. Even if you are living a Godly life, opposition will come.

Who is behind the opposition?

Satan is behind the opposition to believers carrying out Gods plan for their lives. Opposition or persecutions is part of our package deal alongside Salvation.

Through oppression our behaviors are attacked, and our entire life is influenced. If our entire life is influenced this encompasses our personality, our thoughts, our actions as well as our social, emotional, behavioral, financial, and spiritual assets.

Well if I appear a little confused, I am not, but I will say this these things are also effects in possession and according to the Holman Bible Dictionary, demon possession attempts to control to affect our personality. It all seems interchangeable to me with just one area uncovered, the physical body.

Possession is known to fully control the physical body where in the person possessed adopts the voice, the personality and actions of the demon. Well we have been doing that for years. Way before we were saved and many saved still continued to do it today. We all have been spokesmen or women for Satan. We are constantly spouting simple worldly concepts, giving ungodly advice& opinions, spreading lies, gossip and slander. If that is not using the voice of the enemy then I don't what it is.

However, I know we think the voice only has to do with some deep mystical sound wherein your natural voice changes and this can happen but the enemy is much cleverer than that. Someone changing their voice or sound is a dead give a-way. The enemy's voice takes on many sounds. It can sound cunning, kind, even gentle, but you have to look for the fangs in the mouth of the person who speaks.

True story,

One day on my job a young women and I were in an office and the conversation on marriage came about. Upon sharing God's view on the matter to another young lady, this woman spouted out jokingly, watch them jokes, derogatory remark about me, My head turned and asked, *"Silence, by whose authority do you speak?"* Well she was shocked and came to a complete hush instantly. Her face went from a smiley face to a frown face at that statement. She left that room upset. The others just looked at me with puzzled faces. They did not quite understand what had happened, but she and I knew.

Later I am happy to say that this same woman came to my room and made confession of her regressed state with Christ. This did not happen right away for that fact she made it her point to target me through gossip, and other tactics of the enemy. I still showed her kindness anyway.

When you reveal the enemy, he does not like it one bit and will continue to attack, but just remember victory is ours. We win because Christ never loses. If Christ ever loses we are in trouble for sure.

I do not take lightly what people say even jokingly and I am a person who loves to make people laugh. Humor is a good thing if used correctly, however if it is used to take jabs, it can be deadly. God taught me some simple things to do when the enemy seeks to attack me. Ask the question, by whose authority do you speak?

We are so full of leaven that the enemy can use the uncircumcised parts of us as weapons against one another knowingly or unknowingly. If we don't give God our attitude, personality, emotions and those little foxes that stand in the way of our spiritual walk, then the enemy will continue to use those areas against us and others.

Personality contends with the emotional, attitudinal, and behavioral aspects and so if possession involves us adopting the attributes of the enemy we must look at what these qualities of the enemy look like before we can rule them out.

Nowhere in the Bible do we see a greater example of the truth than 1 Corinthians 15:33: Evil communication corrupts good behavior than in the example of Adam and Eve in the garden when Satan communicated with them thereby influencing them to sin against God.

For someone to say that our behavior cannot be influenced by the enemy would mean that they are deceived and believe a lie. Our behaviors are influenced by our thoughts. We act out of what we believe and think. If Satan has control of our thoughts or even dominates a little aspect of it, you better believe we are going to have actions of the demonic spirit that are influencing our mind. We will act just as we think. If the demonic spirit is selfish, we have and will take on that personality especially if we haven't allowed God to deal with us in that area.

Let me ask you this question and be honest. Have you been selfish since your Salvation confession and even after numerous teaching on not being selfish this quality still remain an area in your life that still has a strong hold on you?

One of the characteristics of Satan is rebellion God tell us that our rebellion is as the sin of witchcraft!

We all have rebellion in us. From birth to the grave many remain rebellious. We don't always do what we are told to do by God the way he wants us to do it, me included. If I didn't include myself I would be a liar which is another attribute of Satan, the father of lies which is another name of the devil. He is a liar. It doesn't matter what lie you tell or how you tell it, whether or not you lie every day or once in a while, it is a lie. Thank you Jesus for mercy and grace because we would all be in some trouble.

Unfortunately, we have those in the church who practice the art of lying every day. It makes you wonder doesn't it?

Are you getting the jist of what is being said, if not yet, then pray and ask go to open up your heart to receive His Truth.

Now we have seen the words, possess, control, influence, dominate, own interchange constantly and it should send off a spiritual light bulb as to how demonic forces, evil spirits can gain access to us to possess, but if not I will elaborate further.

CHAPTER 8
FURTHER ELABORATION

Lead by the Holy Spirit, I began to substitute each definition into the original question. For example, if I were to substitute "influence" into this question it would read,

"Can A Christian Be Influenced By Evil Spirits?"

Concerning this new question, I would say yes, we can. According to Ephesians 6:10-20

10 Finally, be strong in the Lord, and in the strength of His might. 11 Put on the full armor of God, that you may be able to stand firm against the schemes of the devil. 12 For our struggle is not against flesh and blood, but against the rulers, against the powers, against the world forces of this darkness, against the spiritual forces of wickedness in the heavenly places. 13 Therefore, take up the full armor of God that you may be able to resist in the evil day, and having done everything, to stand firm. 14 Stand firm therefore, having girded your loins with truth, and having put on the breastplate of righteousness, 15 and having shod your feet with the preparation of the gospel of peace; 16 in addition to all, taking up the shield of faith with which you will be able to extinguish all the flaming missiles of the evil one. 17 And take the helmet of salvation, and the sword of the Spirit, which is the word of God. 18 With all prayer and petition pray at all times in the Spirit, and with this in view, be on the alert with all perseverance and petition for all the saints,19 and pray on my behalf, that utterance may be given to me in the opening of my mouth, to make known with boldness the mystery of the gospel, 20 for which I am an ambassador in chains; that in proclaiming it I may speak boldly, as I ought to speak.

Not only has that, but even in the natural we are influenced by peers, parents, community, environment, politics and so forth. These forces of evil are present in this world and they are influencing not only the world, but the people of God as well. All the philosophies of the word are carnal influences no matter how profound they might seem. Unless they align with God they are to be rejected. I know we don't like that nor do we want to accept that but it does not change it from being the truth of the matter.

God said in Philippians 2:5-8

5 Let the same mind be in you that was in Christ Jesus, 6 who, though he was in the form of God, did not regard equality with God as something to be exploited, 7 but emptied himself, taking the form of a slave, being born in human likeness. And being found in human form, 8 he humbled himself and became obedient to the point of death— even death on a cross.

This should indicate to us that our mind is corrupted with thoughts of a system that is not Godly and under the temporary control of another master, spirit or better yet Satan. Notice that Jesus in verse 7 emptied himself. That is what we are expected to do daily. We leave the altar of our confession still full with corruptible thoughts that must go, otherwise those thoughts will continue to imprison us in our former life and ways of thinking.
.

God said that in the last days many will depart from the faith and be led away captive by seducing (persuading, enticing, luring) spirits. (1Timothy 4:1) Does that sound like we can be under the influence of something other than God? I believe it does.

But this is not where the controversy begins. The

confusion with this question begins when the word "possess" takes on the meaning of ownership or control. Many feel that Christians cannot be owned (possessed) like property by an evil spirit or demon since we have been redeemed with the precious blood of Christ. They feel that we are no longer the property of Satan but Christ so evil can't control us. They feel that we can only be oppressed.

Before I address this, I feel that we need to go back and first clarify first, what "own" "control", and "redeem" means.

Own: to have or hold as property; possess; to have power over; control; to admit.

From the definition we can see similarity to the word "possess" and look there goes that meaning control again. So we can conclude that ownership and control are one in the same.

Secondly, let us look at what the word "redeem (ed)" means. Redeem/ed 1. To buy back; repurchase, b. to get or win back. 2. To free from what distresses or harms (like to be free from captivity or ransom). b. to extricate from or help to overcome something detrimental c. to release from blame or debt; clear; to free from consequences of sin 3.To change for the better 4. Repair; Restore.

Looking at both of the definitions, let us examine what this means in light of what was talked about earlier.

Everyone can agree or at least should, that Jesus came to bridge back the gap that sin put there through our mistake in the garden. Right! Overall, the purpose was to restore us and repair the breach created by sin. This is what Satan stole from us when Adam and Eve fell into sin. The relationship between the creator and the creation was torn apart. What man was given dominion over (the earth) was stolen and now Satan who is the Prince of this World is the lease holder. God wants our relationship repaired and restored. He wants to make us, once again, joint heirs and finally restore man back to his rightful kingship of the earth.

So with that point clear, we come to the second one. What is redeemed by Christ when we enter into Salvation with Him? When Christ died on the cross, He not only took the keys pertaining to life, but also death. So who had the keys?

SATAN did!

Many feel that possession leads to some type of a demonic take over. That the demon can take over our body as he did with Legion. My response is that he sure can. That is definitely the highest level of possession but there are many levels of possession, and that is what we look at further down the road.

Going back to the definition, we can see that possess/ed/ion has more than one meaning. Have you ever tried to explain something to someone but what they understood is not what you truly meant?

Well, that is what we do with God's word. Instead of taking everything back to the Author, we rely on our natural intelligence, reasoning, and logic for an understanding. Only the one who authored the book can truly tell you what He meant. The Bible was written by men but inspired by God. Human error is always a factor that's why we must seek God for the interpretation and we need the Holy Spirit to do it.

In the Old Testament God did not use everyone to interpret what He was saying. There were prophets and judges that God used to tell the people what His will was, but mostly Prophets who also acted as Judges. Is not this how Moses sister Miriam got in trouble with God? She said, "Does God only speak to Moses"?

Apparently He was and what did God do with her for this statement, she ended up with leprosy. Many don't like the message but even greater than that they hate the messengers more. The Jews always killed the prophets. They never wanted to accept what God said through them. Nothing new, we do the same things today because God is sending the prophets after the remnant, His chosen people.

He is moving through the churches now and there is nothing anyone can do about it. Since religion and their religious people have tried to stifle the voice of the prophets in the church, Jezebel and her crew of false prophets are able to move right on in. Many have been trained religiously like the Pharisees and scribes did with the people of Israel. They were afraid to truly believe in Christ for fear of what the religious men would do to them so many of them denied Christ and the Apostles were given the commission to turn to the gentiles.

This is why God is agitated with man. Look at all this confusion over the meaning of words. Choosing the wrong definition can change the whole context of what it was originally meant to express. Don't you just hate it when people misquote you or put words in mouth? That is one of my pet peeves. I would rather you ask me if this is what I meant than to misunderstand and possibly mistreat me for what was misinterpreted.

God asked us to rightly divide the word of truth. How can that be done without the Holy Spirit? How can a theology school or a training school do that? They can give you foundational stuff but the true meaning must come from God. Most theologians and philosophers aren't Holy Ghost filled. They are men who like school, who make themselves a reputation by their degrees and knowledge, although carnal. Just like I can go to school to become a doctor, I can become a teacher of biblical philosophy, a pastor, and so forth but none of it is driven by God. Just like everyone doesn't come to school to learn, some for lunch. Well many are doing just that as part of a system of belief rather than by appointment.

Here I go again opening my big mouth, mouth that the devil has tried to shut for years. Although it should be apparent there are still a few that don't quite understand what I am about to say. However, I do believe that many are slowly but surely coming into this painful realization that we have charlatans in the pulpit.

Yes, Lord, we have wolves in the pulpit (false pastors), snakes in the field (false evangelist), people that see dead people (false prophets), know it all (false teachers), people with no green thumb (false apostles) all around us and many of them are teaching us things that are not truth. It is taught with leaven, lots of leaven. Again we are being slaughtered because we lack discernment and wisdom.

According to the definition if I chose a different meaning of the word possess, the question changes and so does the meaning. This is the point. As much as I love looking and researching topics and their meanings, in the end, it is the Holy Spirit that must interpret it for me and this leads us to the problem and the confusion that God is talking about.

I did all of that to show and make a point. With so many meanings pertaining to just one word, how one decides which one relates to what Christ is saying, my friend is where the problem lies. Many of us have decided what Christ means. We have interpreted his wisdom though logic and education. Most theology schools are filled with professors who teach others based on their common logic, and nothing else.

They prescribe methods to us like how to teach or study the Bible, how to pray and so forth. God gave us the method. He said if anyone needed wisdom or understanding, we are to, ask man or ask Him. Ask God! Jesus left us a teacher, the Holy Spirit. So this take us back to what I stated earlier, how can we all have the Holy Spirit, yet not agree on interpretation.

After all the research we are supposed to take it to God. Only God can tell us what is meant on any subject matter. This is how doctrines of men and fables are born. Man's wisdom and man's interpretation.

If I chose to believe that possess meant, influence then that question then others would agree to that fact, but because it has been interpreted as owed, it makes it harder to believe that as Christian we cannot be possessed by evil spirits. I believe we can!

Believe we don't have the meaning wrong as to why so many of us are walking demon possessed, oh I am sorry demon influenced unaware. This is why many are delivered that way Christ said we should be able to do.

The Bible interchanged the word possession with unclean spirits quite often, and truly that is all a demon is, an unclean spirit. God even speaks to us regarding the effects of having unclean spirit cast out of man and what would happen if the unclean spirit doesn't find any rest. It returns right back to the place it was cast out of and if we have not occupied the space, filled it with truth of God's word then that spirit has the right to reenter and with more. I believe that is what happens to LEGION as to why so many spirits existed. Every time they left more and more came until the hold was so much stronger than the personality of the man.

Matthew 12:43-45 (Amplified Bible)
43But when the unclean spirit has gone out of a man, it roams through dry [arid] places in search of rest, but it does not find any. 44Then it says, I will go back to my house from which I came out. And when

it arrives, it finds the place unoccupied, swept, put in order, and decorated. 45Then it goes and brings within seven other spirits more wicked than itself, and they go in and make their home there. And the last condition of that man becomes worse than the first. So also shall it be with this wicked generation.

We have truly made a mockery of God's word and many of us are guilty of operating in fleshly wisdom and believing it is God. This brings question as to how many of us who say they are filled with the true Spirit of God really are. Or if they are allowing the Spirit to truly lead, guide, and teach them.

Asking for knowledge, wisdom and understanding is easy. Gaining is not, it requires a great deal of patience and perseverance. Many want to rush into it. Give God four days, if that much, before speaking before His people concerning a matter, to tell them his hidden truth. Some truths aren't revealed right away. Sometimes we have to toil with God and wait on Him. We have no idea on how he will bring forth His truth or when. Go tell us that what we know is only a part not a whole and so this book is my part, the part given to me for you.

The bible is a carefully coded book. Reading it like a regular book, page by page, chapter by chapter will give understanding. You are sure to gain the logos form of God's Word which why is what most theologians know, but Rhema is different. We have many how to books on many issues but not all that is written is of God either so we must be very discerning of what we read. God told us to guard what we hear and see.

If we think about the many avenues to hearing and seeing we need to take heed and become more discerning and not take for granted because one says that they are saved they are writing from the Spirit of God. You do know book writing has become a new fad too. If you listen to people, God has told everyone to write a book these days. We all have story to tell but it is more than a story to tell, it is writing for purpose and destiny.

CHAPTER 9
The Meat & the Potatoes

Upon writing this book, I wanted to ensure that the content was 100 per cent accurate according to the knowledge of what God wants us to understand.

Have you ever had a WOW moment? Well, one day while doing my hair, the Holy Spirit spoke something inspirational to me that made me say, WOW! It made everything about this subject matter much clearer and my understanding is forever enlightened by it.

God had made it perfectly clear that I must finish this book. I must confess I had been dragging my feet for a while, but he made it clear that this book must get done now. I had been pulling on the God for several months about this subject matter. So I said to God,

"If you want me to write this book, I must be clear on the books purpose and the point you want me to make in it."

I wanted to know beyond a shadow of a doubt why I was writing this. I knew that this topic was controversial. I knew that it would ruffle the feathers of the theologians and their students. I knew that this would place me under great spiritual attack. If I was going to go through all of this, you better believe I wanted to be right about it. I don't want to do anything especially with God's name attached to it in my own strength or knowledge.

God makes it clear in Hosea 4:6 that his people suffer for lack of knowledge, and we have. Those leaders who knowingly or unknowingly committed heresy will answer to God for it. We have been swallowing the bait of Satan through false leaders influencing Godly doctrine. This has contaminated our religious beliefs system

God has been warning us that there are false leaders in the vineyard. The Parable of the Wheat and Tare growing up together is an excellent example of the mixture of light and darkness not just in the world but in the house of the lord too. People there are false leaders who Satan planted among us to accomplish his mission of confounding them who think they are wise and allowing them who he has confused to spread that venom to those of us who don't know any better.

The Bible say in Mark 14:27-5, "If you smite the shepherd you scatter the flock." God has his own way of disciplining and purifying His flock. If a pastor loses sight of the True Shepherd and forgets that he is an under-shepherd and a steward, he can begin to lead the flock astray. People will begin to follow the man and not the Lord. People will put him on a pedestal and "worship" him. Doesn't this sound like many of us today?

The pastors are gods we have been taught to worship. He is the law. We need his okay. It became a Pastor's autonomy which is not what God intended. We see one man making all decisions and placing around him those who will not challenge his authority. This has been going on

for a long time now and God is sick of it. An upset is upon the horizon. That why you see the race to the top. Pastors moving into what they deem as the highest position, the Apostle!

You know the devil is very clever. More clever than man can ever know. Because of this we have been duped into lies and false doctrines all because of this simple fact that I am about to go into.

The Holy Spirit said, "The enemy aim is to possess us through our mind".

I know, WOW, right! Tell you something that you don't already know. This information may not be new to some, but what God wants us to understand is the method of how Satan is accomplishing this mission is what surprised me. The Holy Spirit proceeded to say,

"Many of us are possessed right now and don't even know it."

That's the part that stunned me the most. We are possessed and don't even know it. How can that be?

Here is another example God gave me. He said many believe that the greatest trick that the enemy has done was by convincing people that he doesn't exist, but that's not the greatest trick. That trick only works on the world because they are blinded from truth, but when you are saved you know that the devil is real and that he exists.

However, the greatest trick, God says, is getting into the mind of God's people, the church folk, through our religious system to control the very religion we so faithfully serve.

That was a "WOW" moment for me too. All I could think about was spies and espionage. I could actually see how the enemy could accomplish this and has been accomplishing this for years.

God said, "In combat if your enemy wants to know the working operations, and strategies of your battle plan, then send spies into their camp". Send them in and let them mingle and appear as us in order to gain access.

What am I talking about, right? I am talking about MIND CONTROL! Now I know that sounds crazy and a little farfetched, but if you think about it, it is not that far fetch from reality as you think.

We can see this method very popular among cults like Jim Jones, Reverend Moon, Satanism and New Age just to name few that have existed and still does. Normally, cults prey among people who are weak minded. Cults find out the weakness of their prey and pounce on them. Catch them vulnerable. God said,

"This is what has happened in the church."

This is what the enemy has been doing for hundreds and thousands of years. He has been in the church for a long while deceiving, controlling, and influencing our religious system. In fact, he has even been on the front line of the development of our religious foundation, religious order and practices, and in interpreting God's Word.

The Holy Spirit said that Satan's greatest trick is planting false leaders in the vineyard. Leaders who are already corrupted and have taken on sheep's clothing to lead us down a misaligned path of religion.

Paul asked the Galatians', "Who has bewitched

you?" Why? Because they had leaders, false leaders who were teaching a doctrine different from what they had been founded and taught on.

This is true today!

This doorway of trickery widened during the time of Constantine who decided that since Christianity was growing rapidly, that it was better to join them. Constantine was well known for being the first Roman Emperor, converted to Christianity. By the time of Constantine's birth, Christianity had been around for a few centuries.

As a community, the Christians were well organized, tightly knitted, rich, and influential, but they were still a minority in the pagan Roman Empire distrusted by the government. Even after repeated persecution of the church it failed to make them conform.

Constantine became a Christian in 312. In 313 Constantine came to an agreement with the Eastern Licinios that resulted in some benefits for Christianity. This included reclamation of property, reimbursement of loses and legal rights in a disputes.

Next Constantine issued a series of legislations that favoured Christian clergy. Churchlands became tax free. The clergy would receive an allowance so that they could focus their energies on serving God. Christians also had permission to obtain help from government officials in building new churches.

Just as some good evolved from his conversion, negative was also imparted. With this new found power, we tend to make gods after our own image.

That's' why Christians focus more on being right than being loving, They are more concerned about passing laws to enslave the people to them than obeying what the Lord said also known to most as RELIGIOUS LEGALISM.

The Roman Emperor Constantine established himself as the head of the church around 313 A.D., which made this new "Christianity" the official religion of the Roman Empire. The first actual

Pope in Rome was probably Leo I (440-461 A.D.), although some claim that Gregory I was the first (590-604 A.D.).

This ungodly system eventually ushered in the darkest period of history known to man, properly known as the "Dark Ages" (500-1500 A.D.). Through popes which are not found in scripture, bishops, formerly known as elders, and priests existed only in Old Testament until Christ our High Priest, Satan ruled Europe, and Biblical Christianity became illegal. Christianity was now being influenced by Constantine, a Roman Emperor who mixed in his former pagan practices with Christianity.

Who has bewitched you?

Henceforth, the foundation of the Roman Catholic Church was born. The Roman Catholic Church claims to have started in Matthew 16:18 when Christ supposedly appointed Peter as the first Pope. However, an honest and objective student of the Scriptures and history soon discovered that the foundation of the Roman church is none other than the pagan mystery religion of ancient Babylon.

If you know anything about the Catholic Church, you would know that their doctrine is mixed with a lot of leaven. They worship idols. They made Mary the mother of Jesus, who was considered to be blessed among all women into a god-like image, a queen. Their practices are agonistic. Their belief has a form of godliness but denies the power thereof.

In the Bible there are no popes or priests to rule over the church. Jesus Christ is our High Priest (Heb. 3:1; 4:14-15; 5:5; 8:1; 9:11), and all true Christians make up a spiritual priesthood (I Pet. 2:5). Jesus Christ has sanctified all Christians who believe on Him (Heb. 10:10-11), so all priest today are unnecessary and unscriptural. Furthermore, the practice of calling a priest "father" is forbidden by Jesus Christ in Matthew 23:9. There is only ONE mediator between God and men (I Tim. 2:5).

The Christian church had changed under the leadership of the Roman Empire. The Bishops and Popes had set themselves up with political power, lived in the lap of luxury and claimed that they were the final authority on all things Christians, which is how many look at them now.

They insisted that all Christians everywhere were under their jurisdiction. At the same time they had taken all the rituals and ceremonies and liturgies of the ancient pagan Roman religions, called them Christian liturgy and insisted that these ceremonies were the heart and reality of the Christian religion.

Let me stop here!

I shared some needed history because I want to make a point that since 313, Christianity took on a new religious look. It no longer looked the way Jesus Christ and the Apostle had set it up to look. This type of sabotage has been going on since then, and still now.

We have to begin to see the point. That the doctrine we follow is contaminated. It has leaven in it. This leaven started before Constantine with people like the Galatians, who became bewitched by false doctrine preached to them. What is true then is true now.

The tactics of the enemy has not changed. He has been planting throughout history, false leaders who came and changed and diverted innocent following people from the truth of God. If you change a little bit here and cut a little bit there, you have a new design, a new idea, a new thought, a new view! You have added and taken away from God's Word, which is a big No, NO!

CHAPTER 10

THE FINALE!

We have been operating through false doctrine. This religious poison has been filtering through the blood stream of the Christian Church world for a long time. This is why we have divisions among us; Different religions with different doctrines and beliefs arguing over the Word of God in regard to what has been taught and what God means. This is how we have been possessed.

What does all this mean in a nutshell? It means that we been drinking contaminated wine, with leaven in our doctrine. God puts it this way. If you affect the way a man thinks, you can control the mind. You convince them that our thinking is right and theirs is wrong. You get them to believe that they should follow what is being taught and sooner or later you have them doing what you want them to do. Muslims do it this way, Buddhist do it this way, and Cults do it this way, so why wouldn't Satan attempt to do Christianity in the same way. The other religions don't see Christ for who He truly is. They are blind. Satan is not concerned with those that are already blind.

Christianity is a threat to Satan because we have Christ, although with a twisted understanding of who God is.

Above all religions we should have known better but how can we, if we do not do what Christ has said: 1. Search the scriptures and see if they are of God. 2. Know them that labour among us. We have dropped the ball and have given way to seducing spirits who have led us into captivity. The captivity involves us performing religious practices in substitute of a real relationship with God.

Throughout the Bible God has warned us of false leaders, but we never thought that we were serving any. Some of us are serving them now and don't know it. We never bring to question, whether these people were sent by the Lord. We just accept and take in whatever is taught to us without question.

True Vision!

God showed me a Bride with her legs wide open.

She was wearing a bride dress but the dress was dirty, torn, and tattered. When I asked God who that was He said, "The Church".

I said, WOW!

What God showed and explained to me was that His Bride, the Church was not prepared to receive the Brides groom which is Jesus Christ as of yet. The gown was torn, dirty and tattered because she was no longer the vision of beauty God had in His plan. When we mingle with the world, play their games their way, practice their traditions and follow their false doctrines, we smell like a filthy rag. We have taken on the look of our captors and what should be a sweet fragrance in the nostrils of God is a nasty stench.

Out of following false doctrines, we have reacted out what we were taught to think. We speak based on what we are taught to think, and believe by what we are taught to think. The Pharisee's teachers and leaders of that time had control over the Jews mind. They knew the logos Word of God but lacked Rhema or understanding. The Jews, although seeing miracles, signs and wonders still wanted Barabbas, the thief instead of Jesus Christ. We are saying the same thing to God. Give us the world and all it holds, it riches, it fame, its beliefs.

We want the Kingdom of this World and the Kingdom of Heaven too! But I hear the Lord Say, "We cannot serve two masters, we must love one and hate the other".

If possession is based on the use of the body and voice of a person then isn't that what we are doing? We may not be throwing up green gook, spinning our heads around, or have a strange change in voice, but we are teaching heresies just as dangerous and deadly. Spreading lies and falsehood about God is doing the same thing. You are saying what Satan wants you to say, which is equal to spreading his lies through our voice in the earth.

You have been convinced that what you believe is right, that your doctrine has the correct understanding of God. What you feel about Christianity is no different than any other religion feels such as the Jehovah Witness organizations.

You can't tell them they aren't the chosen people of God above all. Someone definitely lied to them, and we have been lied to as well.

As long as man is involved the possibility of corruption exists. There is no good thing in the flesh. In the flesh wrong interpretation and errors are possible. The Pharisee's did it then and God says the Pharisees of today are doing it now.

God told us not to put our trust in man. Too many of us have put our trust in a faith, a religion, a doctrine and a man/woman instead of relying solely on the Holy Spirit of God who He, Himself left with us as a comforter, a teacher, our guide in all things pertaining to God. Instead we have substituted education and false theology.

God's Word has been twisted. We have changed what He, Himself, means for power, control, and selfish gain. When I say "we" I am primarily talking to leaders who have been given the responsibility of feeding and tending to the flock of God. We let our guard down. Like Eve, Satan whisper in our ear and makes promises. We bought the lies, hook, line, and sinker.

We have done away with certain principles and laws to fit our own desires. We have led people to believe that Christ is over here and over there when Ichabod, meaning the glory is departed, stands at the door of many who make this claim of Christ.

We don't understand the root to many of these established religions. Most people do not choose their religion it is part of their childhood indoctrination. The Anglican Church was formed as a result of King Henry VII's fight with the Pope over divorce. So King Henry said fine, I'm not catholic anyway and formed his own church. How dangerous!

Why?

The Church belongs to God. It is spiritual, yet we treat it like we try on new shoes. If we don't like the color, the style or the fit we give it back and try on a new one. The Episcopalian religion is a branch of the Anglican Communion both independent of the original Catholic Church. Many religions are founded for many different reasons. Christians have been known for constantly changing and editing the Bible and their religious positions. Check out the root of why yours was founded. For this reason and more we continue to wear a dirty, torn and tattered Brides dress and smell in the spirit.

With our legs gapped open we are susceptible to any and every virus that plagues the earth. We are supposed to guard ourselves by putting on the full armour of God so that we are able to stand against the wiles of the devil. Instead we are getting beat up by Satan, a jealous lover who wants nothing more than to destroy God's beloved, the Church.

We have taken for granted that our leaders are correct and forgot that we have a responsibility in this matter. Put your trust in no man. Bring all to God for divine truth and understanding. Our walk with God is personal and although God provide us with a spiritual government, it does not replace the role of Christ and the Holy Spirit. We listen, and then we investigate, and must gurgitate anything that could be poisonous to our spirit.

So let me bring us back to the purpose of this book. This book was written not to convince you if or if not a person can be possessed. Possess just became the foundation of a bigger problem that has been going on since time began. A problem God wants clarified so that we can begin to examine what we have learned on the road. He wants us to understand that we have been duped. We have been lied to by many who came in the name of God with ill motives. Whose sole intent was to bring confusion, and to enslave us to a form of godliness without power?

Satan does not like God or his creation. He doped us in the Garden of Eden and gained dominion and continues to find ways to make us fall. The question many could have is WHY? Why would God allow such a thing to be done? God did not do it, we did. He left us with the instructions in the Bible. He supplied us with help through the Holy Spirit. He also left us with choices, just like he left with Adam and Eve.

Do not eat from the tree of good and evil? That old slippery serpent, Satan had gotten us to do it the first time in the garden. Satan is still offering us the same enticements which have many of us pilfering people for money, committing all sorts of adultery and fornication in the house. Lying, stealing, power, and control all the worst characteristic of man.

Do not eat from the tree of good and evil? We have taken a bite of fame, and became power hungry. We want our names in light. We want reputation.

Like Paul said, "Though I would do good, evil is present with me, Romans 7:21". Evil is right there looking for an entry and if we give it to him, then it is our fault. God said resist the devil and he will flee. Bind and loose! Put on the whole armour of God, these and more we find in scripture to prevent us from being led astray in all matters of sin against God.

True, no man is perfect and I am far from it myself, but this is not about perfection but about truth and living without excuse for our wrongs. Knowing that God who is just and righteous will forgive us but we must be willing to allow God to crucify our flesh and bring the flesh into subjection to the

Spirit.

We are the woman with the issue of blood (Mark 5:8). We have been bleeding for more than 12 years and we desperately need to touch the hem of Jesus' garment so that we can be made whole. We need to touch him through repentance; Repentance for allowing the devil to dope us. God wants this religious system torn down and that is what he is doing now. What do I mean torn down?

Well, lets me say this. About 10 years ago, God said to me that he was about to do a recall in the spirit. Like a product on the market that is defective, so are some of my children who got duped into ministry too early or are just defective because they haven't let God kill some areas needed for that journey. Right now God is closing some churches down and taking many to be with the Lord. He is coming in church houses and moving His children from among them. Membership for some hasn't budged in months or years. They have the same old people there with a few add-ons here and there, but no real growth. He is shifting the atmosphere!

LESSON BREAK:
Let me say this. Just because someone has a big church doesn't mean that they are always blessed by God. Look at the Catholic Church. They are huge and still their doctrine is agonistic. So in this case size doesn't matter. What matters is who you are serving. Are you serving the true living God or are you just franchising His name but serving low quality meats?

We can get bumper stickers, crosses and tote big bibles. Shout louder than everyone else. Have Jesus' name on the door and still be just as empty as the calories in candy.

Now back to the point.

Jairus' daughter at the same time was dying was also 12 years old. The women having blood issues for 12 years and Jairus' daughter being 12 years old was no coincident. God showed me that both of them were symbolic of two governmental systems, one that needs to be torn down and one that needs to be resurrected.

So Jesus stopped!

The virtuous cries of the righteous have gone forth to God and he has heard our cry. He stopped on the road because he felt virtue come from him. He stopped because of the virtuous cries of His children who have not bowed their knee to Baal. This remnant He is sending to bring what was ailing us to an end so that He can resurrect that which appears to be dying or dead, but is still very much alive.

He wants our minds renewed and corrected to right thinking. He wants the blinders to drop so that we can see correctly. He wants to removes us from the valley and the shadows of death that we have placed ourselves in through disobedience. Like Israel we have been led into captivity by seducing spirits and many still are today.

Unfortunately, some of us will not turn away from the former chains that bind us. They will continue with business as usual. God being judge will deal with them. If we follow the unjust judge we will also reap what they reap, we need to know that. All God wants is for us to return back to our first love which is Him. He wants the church to be of one accord. He wants to flow freely to His bride with open arms without the stench of the world. He wants to wash us and make us white as snow. He wants to remove all spots and wrinkles so he is sending fire. He is removing the viruses from out of our spiritual blood stream.

It is not about being possessed. It is about having a true understanding of God and his ways. It is about having the same mind that was also in Christ Jesus in the church. It is about walking in the likeness of God and all His Glory in the earth.

This is way the enemy is out to sabotage the church so that we will not be all those things and more. God is releasing nuggets from heaven that he so carefully hidden in many you rejected because you thought they were crazy. They did not think like you. They saw through Gods eyes and understood through Gods mind. You threw out the Apostle and the prophet, but they must return. This is why so many are promoting themselves through their false practices to become Apostles. There are so many Apostles popping up these days. Even the cats and dogs are walking around with collars now. That's a joke!

What we need to know is this? We do not have the correct understanding of God's Word nor do we understand His ways because they are higher than ours. We will not obtain this by selling out to the world. Although our gifts come without repentance so many can and are operating on empty. They perform their roles by mimicking God's true anointed one who really don't know who they are either. They are stealing ideas and messages just to keep abreast of what God is saying. This is why networking can be dangerous especially if we can't truly discern by the Spirit.

We need to walk away with the understanding that Words are life and death to God. Since hearing is an avenue that Satan has infiltrated often through music, we need to be careful who feeds us spiritually.

Possession of our thoughts is very dangerous because as a man/women thinks so they are. If what we hear is poison and we don't know it we will believe what we hear, share what we believe as truths, and act out what we believe.

We have been possessed with wrong thinking. Our minds are seared with false doctrine; Doctrine that has a form of Godliness but denies the power thereof.

If Satan get control, influence or possession of your mind and thought then you are a stooge for Him and don't know it. By what you think, you will do!

Many who have been in the church for a while now believes in homosexual marriages? No longer do they feel that God meant marriage to be between a man and women.

Many have created man made system under the name of God for financial gains. There is so much going on right now in the church, I get sick just thinking about it. We have some issues and we need deliverance. We may not bow as a total system but individually God is coming for them who will leave them who want the world and all it has to offer in a reprobate state of mind.

It is my prayer that you get understanding of God and what is written here now.

Now if you want to know what I believe about a Christian being possessed by an evil spirit, I will tell you.

I believe the reverse is true. That we are working to become untangled from the bondage that our former possession of the world system has caused.

I believe the question should be not can we, but how do we become unpossessed by demonic forces that have held us in captivity for so many years of our lives. How do we break the holds, mentality, socially, financially and spiritually that this world has indoctrinated us into.

I believe we came to God possessed. At the altar we take the first step towards transformation process into which God has created us to be, His likeness, His image.

Our transformation takes place when we allow God to renew our minds and reveal to us the evil that is in our hearts. This is when a new heart develops out of a reconditioned mind.

"Therefore, if anyone is in Christ, he is a new creation; old things have passed away-behold all things have become new"
2 Corinthians 5:17

ABOUT THE AUTHOR

A native of the great city of New York, Monique is a devoted mother to four wonderful children (Sierra 20, Tyrone 22, the late Trenton 23 and Renee 28) and grandmother to two beautiful baby girls (Tyese 6 and Alayiah 4 months). She is currently employed in the Baltimore City Public School System as the IEP Chair of one of its divisions of Special Education.

Educated in New York City, she graduated from Adelphi University in 1984 with a Bachelor in

Business Administration with a minor in Psychology, and in 2002 with Masters in Education from Coppin States University, but her greatest accomplishment was in 1989 when she accepted Jesus Christ as her personal Lord and Savior.

Monique has had many spiritual experiences and currently in appointed serve and attendance at Manifested Glory Worship Center under the anointed leadership of Pastor Damon Johnson. She was a member of Living Word Ministries under the anointed leadership of Apostle David H Brown, Monique has served this local assembly by supporting and accepting a leadership role in it auspicious Women's Ministry and she participates as a dancer on it Signs & Wonder dance team.

Prior to her membership at Living Word Ministries, Monique attended Christian Liberty Fellowship under the leadership of Pastors Wesley & Janice McBryde where in 2005 she was ordained into the ministry office of the Prophetess by Apostle Christina Holtclaws and Pastor Carolyn Seawell of East Baltimore Deliverance Church. She also served as an Elder, Administrative Assistant to the Pastors, on the Hospitality Committee, as the Pastor's Aide and Nurse, Choreographer & leader of the Dance Ministry, Media Specialist, and a variety of other committees.

For the past twenty-one years, Monique has dedicated her life to the empowerment and enrichment of others' lives. This is accomplished through her books, speaking engagements and dance. God has blessed Monique with many talents and gifts and she uses them to fulfill the call upon her life.

An inspirational writer and motivational speaker Monique has published and authored two books and has written the forward on another. She is the author of A Father's Love-a poetic book of psalms and Who Is Thy Neighbor-a fiction that explores and reflects on the true heart of the Christian souls. She has written the forward in the book authored by Pastor Trena Stephenson titled, My Secret Garden. She has talked on many motivational topics dealing with the Worth of a Godly Woman, Discovering Your God-Given Gifts, Mirror, Mirror on the Wall, Destiny, Where Are You, and more!

Besides her many services to her local assemblies, through God, Monique has used those talents and gifts to begin her own personal ministry and outreach services. Through the inspiration of the Holy Spirit in 2005, Monique gave birth to a ministry for Women called FirstTouch Ministries for Women (FTMW). FirstTouch Ministries for Women came through the womb with its first Women's conference- "Just a Little Girl Talk". These conferences were built around the community outreach Girl Talk Fellowships that were sponsored for her local community which grew to reach the lives of many others in Maryland, DC and Virginia.

Through FirstTouch Ministries for Women, her desire is to reach out to hurting women as well as disciple them. Spiritual growth is her ultimate goal. Through relational (social, family, communication, witnessing, service, and friendship), physical (health, nutrition, addictions), emotional (self-esteem, depression, crisis', counseling), and mental (decision-making, time management, finances, leadership skills) biblical applications she plans to help them to that desired place of spiritual growth.

In 2008, she began hosting her own online talk show on Blog Talk Radio called The Prophetic Voice for Victory-She Speaks broadcast. Her subject matters are Christian based to promote spiritual growth and bring maturity through prophetically inspired revelation and wisdom (Rhema) from the heart and mind of God. Many of her topics will challenge the body of Christ as she talks about and touch many sensitive Christian issues.

Alongside with the birth of The Prophetic Voice for Victory-She Speaks broadcast came The Prophetic Voice for Victory quarterly eMagazine featuring many inspiring, enlightening, and informative articles stories by anointed men and women of God for men and women of God along with prophetic messages and prophecies, and much, much more.

She has also been the featured guest on the *The Best View's Women's Institute* hosted by the Jean Donnell Ministries, *The Daughters of Distinction: Talk Show* hosted by Pastor Trena Stephenson of The Women of God Ministries, *He's Alive!* Television broadcast, and Show *It's All Talk*

Comcast Television.

Monique graciously draws from the Lord's Spirit motivational messages that will encourage, uplift, enlighten and provide spiritual growth for the soul. Each word written or spoken is an expression of God's infinite wisdom which she obtained from her own trials and tribulation periods. The prayers and anecdotes that she uses to combat her own challenges and the hardships that she faces daily in her life, she now shares with us.

CONTACT INFORMATION

The author would love to hear from you. You can contact the author:

By Email at: www.shespeaks3@aol.com

By Web: Http://www.firsttouch.us

For more life changing messages visit her radio show at:

SHE SPEAKS! The Prophetic Voice for Victory
Http://www.blogtalkradio.com/the-prophetic-voice

You can also find her on "

Face book:
http://www.facebook.com/shespeakswisdom

Twitter: http://www.twitter.com/moemajos

Other Books by The Author Can Be Found On

http://www.Amazon.com

A Father's Love

You know the old saying, "When it rains it pours!" Let me help you out of your storms with my book titled" A Father's Love." A book of inspiring prophetic poetry that will encourage, uplift, and quicken your soul. This paperback book has 126 pages filled with over 60 poems and 15 scriptures to enrich and enlighten your life. Each poem will renew your mind, uplift your heart, and delight your soul. The question that remains is, "Are you REALLY ready to be blessed?"

Who Is Thy Neighbor?

This profound books takes a real hard look at the heart of the Christian soul and the role the Church should take in retrospect to being a good neighbor and a Good Samaritan. This book is centered around the parable of the Good Samaritan, depicts the life of a fiction character named Jasmine to illustrate how to be a good neighbor to one another. Read about Jasmine's seasons of change. See how God moves her from isolation to revelation. Test your own heart and see where you lie. A 206 page power packed book of knowledge you won't want to pass up. Included in the book is a study guide.

www.ingramcontent.com/pod-product-compliance
Lightning Source LLC
Chambersburg PA
CBHW071121090426
42736CB00012B/1970